THRILLING TELANGANA

CANDID CULTURE AND CUSTOMS

KONDA MURALI

ISBN 979-888521893-1

I dedicate this book to the people of Telangana, whose quality is the strife. They always fight to get back what they lose. I also dedicate this book to the honourable chief minister, Shri. Kalvakuntla Chandrashekar Rao garu and our MLA and minister Kalvakuntla Tharaka Rama Rao garu.

Contents

Contents

Contents

Contents

Contents

Foreword

I feel very proud to have Konda Murali, PGT English in our society. And I feel very proud of his achievements in English Literature. I hope his books will be helpful to our students in enhancing communication skills.

B. Shafiulla

The Secretary

TMREIS

Preface

I always want to show my gratitude to my place where I was born and brought up. Since my childhood, I have been observing my place, I felt that it was deserted and no one would represent my constituency (Rajanna Siricilla). I am astonished, seeing the sudden positive changes in our constituency. Everywhere in the state, the topic is about the development and the leader, KTR. I feel very happy for the wide roads, canals and other infrastructure development in our area. I also feel joyous for our dynamic leader who represented his constituency and the state in a very well manner.

I am also very happy for the positive changes in the state after it is separated. Its culture, dialect, clothes, cuisines and all the other aspects are revived. Now Telangana songs, cuisines and dialect are very famous throughout the country. The government decided to make Golden Telangana in all aspects. These things came into my mind and I decided to contribute something from my part. So I have written this book, Thrilling Telangana- Candid Culture and Customs. The book has 108 poems. Each poem depicts the greatness of Telangana and its people. I hope you read the book and aware of the state's grandeur.

Acknowledgements

I would like to acknowledge this book to myself as I am always passionate about writing. And I am self-motivated with my life's situations. Without caring the reputation and money, I keep on writing the books according to my thoughts.

About the writer

Konda Murali is a writer and working as PGT (English) at Telangana Minorities Residential School, Jangaon. He has written twelve books including this book and ten research articles in English language and literature so far. Previously he worked as an Assistant Professor for eleven years in reputed engineering colleges in Hyderabad, Telangana.

His books' list:

1. Bitter Sweet Juices- Life teaches you
2. Forget and Forgive-To reconcile
3. A Book on English Literary Terms – For the literary fraternity
4. The Racharla Fort- Unveiling the history
5. The Pearls of Life- Universal Sonnets
6. The Profound Emotions- Various aspects of humans
7. Lockdown Stories- Impact of Social media
8. The Real Dreams- Reoccurrences of life
9. Love and Life- Quarantine Poems
10. The Ramayan- Balakanda
11. Ayodya Kanda- Sinful exile of Srirama
12. Thrilling Telangana- Candid Culture and Customs

1. The dream came true

When I was a child, I used to dream

I used to dream about my village

If it had a canal, I used to swim

But everywhere, I found sewage

Sometimes I used to travel by trains

I used to see villages from its window

I saw the children jumping into canals

Their happiness was like an overflow

After many years, I recalled my dream

The dream turned into the reality

I am happy for my MLA, Tarak Ram

He arranged for us the cannel facility

Meaning:

During my childhood, I used to feel very bad about our village's surroundings. I used to see beautiful locations when I travel to other places. I saw merry men playing at the bank of the river and children playing in the canals. I used to show my jealous on them. We had not any canal facility but after Telangana is formed, our MLA, KTR concentrated on our area. He made it possible to the area with full of canals. The most astonishing thing is the ground water level rose up to six meters. Now everyone has to see our area.

2. Mission Kakatiya

I was wondered, why are our soils not fertile?
I came to know that ours is a high terrain
I thought that our lands wouldn't propel
I forwent that nobody can strengthen
Something incredible thing happened
Our lands suddenly turned into fecund
as if someone used a magic wand
And the cinematic thing has happened
The reason is Telangana State is formed
The Mission Kakitaya restored all tanks
Mid-Mannair is also swiftly constructed
The credit goes to KCR, KTR, the leaders

Meaning:

It was said that Telangana's soils are not fertail. Even some people argued that geographical boundaries are the reason for that. They said that it was impossible to change the soils into fertail but C.M KCR's idea of constructing Kaleshwaram project, changed the whole scenario. Water is found everywhere now in Telangana. The Mission Kakatiya has become pride of India now.

3. Telangana's Royal Roads

All roads lead to Rome is a proverb
But our roads didn't lead anywhere
That is why, we used to diatribe
The uneven roads made us poorer
Now, our roads are to travel and look
We felt like, we were in foreign
There was no sign of cul-de-sac
All villages are connected to the town
Our MLA, KTR has a broader vision
and worked with a proper mission
He knew, developing roads can save time
They can make the area as a paradigm

Meaning:

The condition of roads were horrible before Telangana was formed. It took more time to reach the destinations. After the state is formed, the government concentrated on the roads. Now one can see the wide roads in nook and corner of the state.

4. Rajanna Siricilla

Nobody knows about our district
There were none to represent it
The people wanted to see their
leader in assembly but no result
The place waited for an efficient leader
After many years, it found our KTR
Now, it's a reputed place in the map
It's moving ahead by great leadership
There were no ministers in the cabinet
Now, our leader is minister, president
His eloquence made the place significant
His efficiency made his people prominent

Meaning:

No one was aware of our district, Siricilla before. And there was no efficient leader to represent our people in the assembly. The people used to feel very bad about their leaders for not highlighting their problems. After KTR became our MLA, it was like sudden unsual thing happened. It is the constituency's boon for KTR is its leader. Now not only in assembly, the constituency got international fame.

5. From Ridiculous to Revolt

Telangana dialect was ridiculed

It was used by the comedians in movies

The cuisines were also grimaced

Even, Telanganites forgot our varieties

They were treated as alcoholics

And they were called as innocents

It was a saying, "No good leadership"

And nobody can save from hardship

KCR made the unattainable attained

He made the state utopian into reality

Now the dialect, cuisines are revered

The traditions got a lot of popularity

Meaning:

Before Telangana is formed our language, our food, our culture and everything is ridiculed. We used to be treated that were men for nothing. You see the change now. Telangana dialect is popular, its cuisines got worldwide popularity and its people are very clever in choosing their leader.

6. Our towns in Telugu Movies

Guntur, Kurnool, Krishna and Vizag
are only the cities, shown in movies
So I thought those were promising
But I had a doubt, Why not our cities!
I knew all movie makers weren't locals
They mentioned only their places
Though the most of audience are ours
There was no importance for places
The whole scenario has been changed
after Telangana State has been formed
Now the change in films is to be watched
Our technicians, places are highlighted

Meaning:

The movie makers used to only their towns in the films. I used to feel very surprised why our villages and towns were not mentioned. And I thought our places had no importance. The towns which had shown in movies are the great. But after Telangana is formed, our towns are being shown.

7. The suicides of weavers

I read the suicides' news diurnal
The news used to surprised us
because it was from same locale
I was surprised about the deaths
The suiciders were Siricilla weavers
They were killed by the unfair policies
The hustles and bustles stopped
Everywhere the despair prevailed
There is no sign of any plight now
The woes of weavers are doomed
KTR stood always by them anyhow
TRS schemes kept them contented

Meaning:

Almost everyday, I used to read the death news of Siricilla weavers in the news papers. The unfair policies killed them but after the state is formed their worries have gone since the government is encouraging them in many ways.

8. Kaleshwaram project- our pride

Kaleshwaram project is our achievement
It is one of the world's largest projects
We heard that projects never complete
But it definitely is not the case with this
CM, KCR's dream project is built swiftly
Younger state could finish it successfully
The gigantic machines amaze us greatly
It lifts and carries water with much safety
The grandiose can't describe the project
It doesn't lift water but it lifts the river
It prevents the wastage and stores it
The water is available even in the summer

Meaning:

Kaleshwaram project is one of the world's largest lift irrigation projects. The technology and gingatic machines used in it amaze the world. The projects are started but they never complete but here the most astonishing thing is the project is completed in very less time by the government. It fills with water almost all the resoirvors and tanks in Telangana. It is the pride of India.

9. A Story of our C.M

On the way to my village from Siddipet,

I always see the Village, Chinthamadaka

I ride my car very slow at that moment

I tell my children, the place is phenomena

When they ask me about the village

I proudly told them, it is a native of KCR

They wondered and they have an urge

to see him whom they read in news paper

We resumed our journey discussing

about him and his great achievements

My children felt very proud of having

the inspiring leader very near to us

Meaning:

We go to our village from Hyderbad. On the way, we have to cross a village named Chinthamadaka. It is the village of C.M KCR. When I shared that with my children, they were astonished. The CM whom they see in the TV is the great leader. When they saw his village, there was no bound to their happiness.

10. The unique Hyderabad

Hyderabad has a historical scene
The monuments reflect its culture
It is a wonderful place to live in
It gives the people a loving gesture
The unique arid climate is pleasant
Love of its people makes warmth
The cost of living here is moderate
The masses are the city's strength
Now it is famous for the technology
The credit goes to KTR's ideology
Its other pearl is Telugu film industry
Hence it's called as cosmopolitan city

Meaning:

Hyderabad is the most unique city in the world. It is a wonderful place to live in. Its moderate climate is the special advantage for the people. The multi-culture of Hyderabad is not found anywhere in the world. And recent years the city has got popularity for Information Technology. That credit goes to KTR.

11. The Brave Bheem

Komaram Bheem was a great leader

He protested Nijam's courts and laws

He made his people brighter, braver

by fighting with Nizam Nawab's soldiers

He saw the pathetic condition of Gonds

Though he was not much educated,

he became the statesman for the locals

Adivasis treated him as a demigod

He gave the slogan Jal, Jameen, Jungle

It means the forest owns to Adivasis

Jodeghat recalls his strife and struggle

His anniversary recollects his boldness

Meaning:

Komaram Bheem was the rebellious leader of Telangana. He saw the pathetic conditions of the gonds. He noticed the unfair laws of Nijam. He bravely fought against the law and made his people braver. His slogan, "JAL, JAMEEN, JUNGLE" was very famous. It means the forest resources belong to aadivasis.

12. Milad Un Nabi

Milad Un Nabi falls in sacred Rabi
It is the birth day of prophet PBUH
The people compose songs, poetry
They also preach and give speech
The birthday is holy day and holiday
as the people were on fast whole day
They do alms to the poor on this day
It is day of memorable history's portray
The people also wear green clothes
as the colour is symbol of paradise
Group meals is offered in mosques
Various exhibits are shown to persons

Meaning:

Milad-Un-Nabi falls in the month of sacred Rabi which is one of the months in Islamic Calendar. The festival is celebrated on the birthday of the prophet, PBUH. The central government declared holiday on the festival. On this day, Muslims do alms to the poor and they listen to the preaches in the mosque.

13. Dussehra brings euphoria

Dussehra brings plethora of euphoria
It makes the people to feel nostalgia
Men merrily move onto the mountain
to see and clap at roller bird of Indian
Dussehra is called as "festival of victory"
It sends off people's worry and misery
The people perform dancing and singing
and burn the effigy of Raavan at evening
Dussehra teaches, "Virtue conquers evil"
Believing in this, People bear hurdle
They feel, "One day we'll definitely win"
The hope becomes their great weapon

Meaning:

Dussehra in Telangan brings a lot of happiness. The people who settled in the cities, feel nostalgic. They remember how they enjoyed on Dussehra. They move onto the mountain and clapping at the roller bird. They exchange the greeting by giving the jambi leaves on this day. The people feel this day throws their problems away and brings victory.

14. The biggest flower festival

Bathukamma is the festival of aroma

The aroma fulfils desire of the women

The women sing songs for the godess

The godess returns to life as Parvathi

Parvathi is the symbol of pure love

Love of the girls turn into marriage

Marriage purifies of their hearts

Their hearts crave for longevity of spouses

Spouses live happily celebrating the festival

The festival thus brings a lot of hope

Hope of positivity prevails throughout life

Life gives chances to be happy in many ways

Meaning:

Bathukamma is the biggest flower festival in the world. The smell of the flowers fulfils the desires of the women. On this day, the women make Bathukamma with different wild flowers. They treat it as the godess Parvathi. They sing folk songs about their by going around it. The godess Parvathi is the symbol pure love. The pure love turns into the marriage and the marriage purifies the heart. The hearts crave for the welfare of their husbands. The festivals give chances to the people to be happy in many ways.

15. Muharram- the sacrifice

Muharram is the first month for Islams

It is second sacred month after Ramzan

It is the day of mourning for the martyrs

The Karabala battle killed Imam Hussain

So warfare is forbidden in this month

The people are on fast, having the faith

and do prayers being away from mirth

It will be done until Ashura, day of tenth

On this day, forceful migration was done

for spreading Islamic message in the region

Even prophet did not escape from migration

He came back to Mecca after the win

Meaning:

Muharram is the first month in the Islamic Calendar. It is the second second sacred month after Ramzan festival. Moharram is the day of the sacrifice. Imam Hussain was killed in the Karabala battle. So It is decided to enagage in the war is forbidden in this month. The people on this day are on the fast. Ashura is the tenth day in the month. To spread the message of Islam, the people were forced to migrate. Even the prophet did not escape from this.

16. Telangana- the brave

O speak Telangana the brave
O praise the soldiers of the state
Feeling so proud recalling how
you detached the darkness
Still sensing the pain you bore
in prisons and in hospitals, that
brought us this state and now
the flag freely waving in the air
The state's glory now you would
have seen, the prominence it has
got around the world, it is at liberty
because of the self sacrifice of thee

Meaning:

Telangana is famous for its braveness. In the history, you can observe the their braveness. The people have been fighting with the evils. They fought with the unjust laws of Nijam. And when their was shunned, they fought with the central government. Finally they got what they wanted with their braveness. But the state lost so many brave people. The poem is saluting and recalling their bravaness.

17. Telangana-our native land

Telangana is our native land
It is patriotic and courageous
The state shines with its candid
hearts of the kind individuals
It has become strong and free
after decades of relentless strife
The state's glory and liberty
made its people live with relief
God blessed the glorious state
to live long with the freedom
Telanganites are now fortunate
to live in culture of humanism

Meaning:

Telangana is our native land. The jewel of the state is the kind heart of the people. The state is free now after the decades of strife. The god blessed the people, giving their freedom back. Now the people are enjoying their freedom.

18. Telangana- Sacred land

The people are blessed to live
in sacred land as it is a place
of bountiful folks, architects
festivals, cuisines and dances
Telangana is a land of multi
qualities, its dialect, art, craft
people and culture is very famous
in the country and in the world
The land always represents for
its magnificent fight and inspiration
for future generations, may
the state bright in fame forever

Meaning:

The people are feeling very happy to live in Telangana beacuse the state is glorious place. The state has the culture of folks, festivals, cuisines, ancient dance forms and the beautiful architecture. The dialect is so famous in the country. The way of the people's fight will definitely be a inspiration to the future generations.

19. Ask the fort of Warangal

Ask the fort of Warangal
to know the braveness of Telangana
Enquire the fort of Golkonda
it answers you the greatness of it
Visit Yadadri and Vemulawada
to know the sacredness of the state
Go to Medaram and Nagoba fair
they recollect you Kumbamela
Celebrate Bathukamma and Bonalu
to know the exquisite of the state
Go on a tour to Kunthala and Pakala
they exhibit you the beauty of it

Meaning;

Go and ask the fort of Warangal to know the braveness of Telangana. To know the greatness of it, enquire the Golkonda fort. Visit Yadadri and Vemulawada to know its sacredness. Go to Medaram and Nagobha, they will recollect you Kumbhamela. Celebrate Bathukamma, you will feel the grandeur of Telangana. The poem depicts, everything in the state will tell you about the greatness of the state.

20. My Telangana

Oo.. Telangana Aa.. Telangana
My Telangana Our Telangana
I sing the prominence of you, My Telangana..
You not a place but the way of living the life
Your people are the models in leading the life
You are the pride for the art and culture
which flourished hundreds of years ago
Your dialect is praised in the country and
the architecture lauds the culture of you
Your sons, Pothana and PV Narasaimha Rao
proved the greatness of their mother
The festivals, Bathukamma and Bonalu
Depict your daughters' life

Meaning:

Telangana tells the other states and nations, how to live the life. The way, the people lead their lives is so nice. You can't find anywhere in the world. The poets, leaders, festivals and so many things brought good name to Telangana.

21. Yadagiri- the state's sanctity

Yadadri yearns to expand its sanctity

Yardage has turned into acreage

Temple decides to be extraordinary

It wants to be famous for pilgrimage

Telangana needs a temple like Tirumala

KCR's dream to build equalled Tirumala

The dream became true in four years

with the hard work of many sculptures

The uniqueness is to use black granite

We hardly aware of gigantic investment

It's built according to shasratas of ancient

The work recalls the Kakatiyan's architect

Meaning:

Yadagiri decided not only to expand its temple area but also to expand its sanctity. In Telangana, it is the only famous pilgrimage center like Thirupathi in Andra Pradesh. KCR, our chief minister decided to make it famous. Thus the small temple now has expanded to many acres. The architecture of it is a special attraction to the temple.

22. Vemulawada- The pride of Chalukya

Telangana's addenda with Vemulawada
Once it was the capital city of Chalukya
Now it's famous for god Raja Rajeshwara
It's the most famous temple in Telangana
The lord Shiva is called here as Rajanna
So KCR made the district Rajanna Siricilla
It is treated as South Indian's Varanasi
Yearly there's a celebration of Shivarathri
Poet Bhima is associated with the place
So it has also the historical prominence
Honourable KCR also concentrated on this
Lord Shiva as Bhola Shankar, blesses

Meaning:

Telangana has a strong relationship with Vemulawada. It was once the capital city of Chalukya. It is one of the most famous temples in Telangana. The god here is Rajanna. On his name, the chief minister made the new district Rajanna Siricilla. It is called as the south Varanasi. Shivarathri festival is celebrated grandly here. Poet, Bhima was associated with the temple. Shiva as Bola Shankar blesses the people.

23. Bhadradri Ramaiah

Bhadradri has link with the Ramayana

Once it was a part of Dandakaranya

During exile lord Rama built Parnasala

It was here, Ravana abducted Sita

It thrills the pilgrims with its sanctity

It recalls the episodes from Ramayana

Ramadasu built the temple and city

For this he spent in jail in the Golkonda

It is treated as South India's Ayodhya

We are fortunate to have in Telangana

Every year, Rama Navami is celebrated

We visit the temple and are blessed

Meaning:

Bhadradri is a place associate with the epic, Ramayana. The crucial event, the anduction of Sita by Ravana had taken place here. When you visit the place, you will be thrilled. It recalls the episodes of the Ramayana. The folk singer, Ramadasu belongs to the place. He built the temple without taking the permission of Nijam. For that he was imprisoned later released. Srirama Navami, the birth day of Lord Rama is celebrated grandly here.

24. Rythu Bandhu-A great scheme

Rythu Bandhu is the farmers' boon
KCR is the first CM to begin the scheme
Twice a year, financial help is given
Many farmers are happy with the scheme
Rythu Bandhu means "Friend of Farmer"
It is CM. KCR's the best scheme forever
No one would launch this in the country
TRS govt only thought for the peasantry
Many barren lands turned into potent
as it gives money at the time of sowing
It prevented taking money for interest
Thus it's interesting and supporting

Meaning:

Rythu Bandhu, KCR's scheme is a boon to the farmers of Telangana. He is the first C.M to launch such schemes in India. Yearly twice, the amount is deposited in the banks of the farmers. That amount is encouraging to them in the cultivation od their lands. With this many barren lands turned into fertile. Now KCR is called as the friend of farmer.

25. The poor's dream house

Own house is a dream for a lay man
Dream remains dream for many men
because it's not so easy to make it own
It takes lifetime for an ordinary man
KCR launched Double Bedroom Scheme
The poor's dream has become blossom
The primary need is fulfilled by the CM
For the country, it is the best paradigm
KCR made the poor to live with dignity
All the yester years were with no security
The beneficiaries of 2BHK are very happy
TRS and KCR is the poor people's bestie

Meaning:

The poem is about double bed room scheme, launched by C.M KCR. For everyone, own house is a dream but in the real life constructing it is very hard for an ordinary man. Thus dream remains as the dream. But the scheme of TRS government filled happiness in the many poor families. They now are living with dignity.

26. Kalyana Laxmi

Daughter is a burden for a poor family
They always think about her marriage
The family head work hard with anxiety
To reduce tensions, KCR gave a package
Kalyana Laxmi's for Hindu lower group
Shaadi Mubarak's for Muslim section
The schemes provide financial help
The family can reduce their burden
TRS govt gives good support to the girls
There is no worry about the daughters
Telangana is a state, takes care of these
Telangana concentrates on all aspects

Meaning:

Everybody feels that daughter is a burden to the family. From her birth, They think about her marriage. It is very difficult get their marriage for the poor. For them KCR has launched Kalyana Laxmi for Hindu families and Shaadi Mubarak for Muslim families. Thus KCR has become the father of the brides and reduced the burden of the poor.

27. Asara Pension- boon to the old

Asara pension is for vulnerable section
It is launched to live life with dignity
Life's tough in the world of competition
It provides basic needs to the needy
Society's duty to take care of its people
So TRS government started the scheme
The amount is more and it is very useful
The needy overcome from their problem
KCR has become an elder son to the old
TRS govt is very close to the poor family
Scheme got acclamation from the world
It is said, "CM's ideology is revolutionary"

Meaning:

The old are shunned by their sons and daughters. It is common sight to see that the rich are putting their parents in the old orphanage. We can think of the situation in the poor families. Life has become tougher for the young and what about the poor old people. KCR became their elder son by launching Asara Pension scheme.

28. Harithaharam

Environment keeps away from ailment
Forest makes environment complete
If we destroy it, we can't bear its retort
One and only solution is to protect it
Harithaharam is started to rejuvenate it
Its primary aim is to expand the forest
Afforestation is promoted through it
The project protects the state's habitat
Crores of plants are planted in the state
Within few years, it's changed the site
Many accolades, the government got
It's become the model for the planet

Meaning:

The first and foremost priority should be given to the environment. It keeps us away from all the ailments. If we destroy it, there will no future to the human kind. So in the part of protecting it, TRS government has started Harithaharam Program to expand the forest. In this program, every years crores of saplings are being planted. For this the government has won many accolades.

29. A young I.T minister

A young IT minister is a man of witty
He keeps on wondering with his work
He transformed Hyd into a unique city
IT business is developed by Rao Tarak
Crossing nepotism he proved himself
He is real model for a capable leader
Personally he has ambitions in his life
though his father is leader and orator
Apple, Google, Infosys and Amazon
Like these many MNC's are set up
Hyderabad became a software region
After USA, now Telangana is in the top

Meaning:

Taraka Rama Rao has become IT minister at the early age. He is young but his actions are like the experienced. Though he came into politics as a son of KCR, he proved himself. His oratory and leadership skills stood him as a leader. In short span of time, he transformed Hyderabad as a big IT hub.

30. Ancient folk arts

Telangana has various folk art forms
Yakshagana and Chindu are famous
These are mixed with music and dance
They received patronage and finesse
Perini is very old form of dance
It is also known as dance of warriors
Oggu katha, Golla suddulu are some others
These are stories of developed traditions
Dhoom Dham is art form of dance and songs
They clearly depict the people's struggles
Telanganites adopted many art forms
These are different with place and case

Meaning:

Telangana is very famous for folk arts. Yakshagana and Chindu are very ancient folk arts. These are performed with music and dance together. Like these there are many folk arts like Perini, Oggu Katha, Golla Suddulu. These stood Telangana in the nation. The recent Dhoom Dhaam played a vital role in winnig Telangana.

31. Gurukulam

Gurukula is KCR's daughter of mind
He started nine hundredan schools
The schools are for underprivileged
These are all English medium schools
For BCs Mahatma Jyothibha Pule
For SCs and STs Social Welfare
For Minorities, Minority Residential
And for all there is a general society
Thousands of teachers are employed
Lakhs of poor students are educated
The schools are model for the world
as quality is meeting the global need

Meaning:

Gurukula schools are running successfully in the state. There are about nine hundredan schools are established for different strata. In them, lakhs of poor students are styding. They are providing corporate facilities to the students. Gurukulam is KCR's daughter of mind.

32. Kaloji-people's poet

A poet made his name in the history

He is well known as people's poet

His poems inspired Telangana society

Kaloji Narayana Rao is that poet

His slogans tell, "Country is important"

His poems speak, "Humans are great"

His stories convey, "Live life to the fullest"

His life expresses, "Fighting is his spirit"

His literary works are in many languages

He received many numbers of accolades

TS State started a university on his name

He spent his life was with strife and optimism

Meaning:

Kaloji was a great poet of Telangana. He made his name in the history. He is called as people's poet. His literary works inspired the people of Telangana in many ways. He wrote in many languages and received many awards.

33. Saraswathi's son

A Telugu man got fame to his country

He knew eighteen languages of India

He is an apple of eye to deity Saraswathi

He is also the first PM from South India

He's our scholar PM.PV Narasimha Rao

PVN is the father of economic reforms

Globalization got its fame by PVN Rao

He held many degrees and positions

He wrote and translated many books

Sahasra Phan is one among them

He can conduct eight fold avadanas

He energized the ballistic programme

Meaning:

P.V Narasimha Rao brought reputation to India in the world. He is affectionate son of the godess, Saraswathi. He was the first person to become Prime Minister from South India. Many economic reforms are made by him. He can speak and write in eighteen languages and he wrote many books too.

34. The Racharla Fort

Racharla Fort is situated in Yellaredypet
It is the historical place of prominent
Vassal king, Singamaraju ruled the fort
I'm very fortunate to be a resident near it
There are many beautiful locations
Singa Samudram's waterfall is famous
Jakkula Cheruvu is jewel to the place
Sathapirilu throws away the miseries
Vinayaka has been gotten out recently
You also feel so excited to see Nandi
The artefacts can be seen in proximity
Racharla Fort craves for an identity

Meaning:

Racharla Fort was once situated in Yellareddypet Mandal of Siricilla district. It has a great historical prominence. It was ruled by Singamaraju, the vassal king of Kakitaya Kingdom. I feel very happy that my village is very near to it. Singamaraju had dug Jakkula Cheruvu and Singa Samudram for the irrigation purpose. In the recent times, lord Vinayaka was unearthed. And Sathapirilu is a famous secular devotional spot.

35. Indelible quality of India

Nonviolence is indelible quality of India
Many tried like Turkish, Queen Victoria
But the trait was spread in the world media
So the people of India were with euphoria
It solved many problems in the country
Separate Telangana State is one of them
The movement recalled Gandhi's ideology
The people got the state without radicalism
Like the Indian noncooperation movement,
Telanganites did against central government
All professionals and farmers came onto
the roads, protested for achieving their state

Meaning:

Nonviolence is the indelible quality of India. Many nations tried to rub the quality. Indians solved many of their problems using Nonviolence. Recent example is Telangana separation. Now the quality is the model for other nations.

36. Telangana- a new civilization

Mother Telangana is a symbol to its civilization
The mother is also an emblem to strife, language
The poet Dasharathi's thought formed into image
He said, "My state is crores of gems studded violin"
KCR brought Mother Telangana into limelight
It filled patriotism in the people towards the state
Using it, they started participating in the movement
And they finally acquired the separate state
Mother Telangana holds Bathukamma in left hand
She holds corn, regional crop in her right hand
Kohinur, Jakab diamonds are studded in her circlet
Her sari and other jewels are replica of local art

Meaning:

Mother Telangana is a symbol to the state's civilization. Her form is an emblem to strife and language. Even Dasharathi told that his state is the violin which is studded with crores of gems. When KCR started Telangana movement, the patriotism again came out from the people. Every part in Mother Telangana indicates something related to the state.

37. The father of Telangana

Prof. Jayashankar's name is symbol of optimism

He fought for the separate state for lifetime

Though he is a child, he spoke against Nizam

In college, he participated in Mulki Program

As a Lecturer, Jayashankar did not remain silent

With his experience, he told his students to agitate

He actively participated in Idly Sambar movement

He also pleaded the intellectuals to contribute

He completed Ph.D and grew up to higher positions

He authored many articles and research journals

To support Telangana, he started many organizations

And he played a key role in forming the party, TRS

Meaning:

Prof. Jayashankar is the father of Telangana. He fought for separate Telangana for his lifetime. In school, in college, in university and at the work, he relentlessly strived for Telangana. He was a part of the first and second phase of Telangana movements. And he played a key role in forming TRS party.

38. Palkuriki Somana

Palkuriki Somana penned classics
He wrote them in many languages
All of his poems were in couplets
His works talk about social customs
He is a follower of Lingayath, Basava
Basava Puranam describes Lord Shiva
It had become the epic for Shaiva
Bheema translated it into Kannada
Panditaradhya Charita is about Music
The conflicts are mentioned in the epic
His poems are melodic and rhythmic
The people of Telangana feel terrific

Meaning:

Palkuriki Somana wrote many classics in many languages. All of his poems are in couplets (two lines). The most of his works are about social customs. He is the devotee of Lord Shiva and follower of Lingayath. Lingayaths worship Basava. Basava Puranam is an epic to them. Poet, Bhima translated it into English. Somana's other epic is Panditaradhya Charita which is about Music.

39. Sarvai Papanna-Telangana king

Sarvai Papanna was a great rebel

He was against caste discrimination

He married a lady who wasn't to his level

He had opposed Zamindari pattern

Moghals tried to conquer on his fort

But he bravely fought with the gang

Later, he invaded on the Warangal Fort

He announced himself as the king

He supported the farmers later

He could formulate a big brigade

And he raided on the fort of Bhongir

But it wasn't successful as the old

Meaning:

Sarvai Papanna was rebellious leader of Telangana. He fought against caste discrimination. To prove that, he married a lady who belonged to lower caste. He bravely fought against Mughals and even with Nizam. He announced himself as a king He was defeated at Bhuvanagiri Fort.

40. Bammera Pothana

A Brahaman from Bammera wrote Bhagavatha

He is passionate, praiseworthy Pothana

He has been the pride of terrific Telangana

His poems always are with phenomena

Pothana was a great devotee of lord Srirama

He was a poet under the king of Rachakonda

The king's name was Shree. Padma Nayaka

The scholar king wrote Rudranavasudhakara

Padma Nayaka had asked eagerly Pothana

to dedicate to him, the epic, Ramayana

But Pothana dedicated the great Ramayana

to himself, without dedicating to Padma Nayaka

Meaning:

Bammamera Pothana wrote Bhagavatha. Pothana was the pride of Telangana. He was a great devotee of Lord Rama. The king, Padmananayaka asked to dedicate Ramayan to him but Pothana refused. The Ramayan which was written by Pothana, dedicated to himself.

41. The courageous women

Women of Telangana are courageous
The queen Rudramadevi is an example
After her, Chakali Ilamma is audacious
For the others, these two became model
Ilamma fought ferociously with feudals
They were cruel Deshmukh and Razakar
Her strife against Nizam was momentous
So people treated her as freedom fighter
Ilamma was born in Washerman's caste
She freed the labourers from free labour
Though the Zamindaris did not support
She had decided to continue agriculture

Meaning:

Telangana women are courageous. The queen Rudramadevi is an example. After her, there were many in the history. Chakali Ilamma has got that importance. She fought ferociously against Jamindari system, though she was an uneducated.

42. Sinare- a great poet

•42•

C.Narayana Reddy was Telangana's dear son
As a Telugu poet, he made his land proud
He won many awards for his literary contribution
His book titles are so creative and privileged
C. Narayana Reddy was replica of multi-talented
He was a translator, actor, writer, lyricist and bard
The most famous prize Gnanapeet was awarded
For films, he penned the songs of three thousand
Vishwambara is about man's journey in the universe
You will be mesmerized and awestruck with it
Nannu Dochukunduvate song is the most famous
Rim-jim Rim-jim Hyderabad song will be ever hit

Meaning:

C. Narayanareddy is the great contemporary poet from Telangana. As a Telangana poet, he made his land proud. He won many awards and rewards for his literary contribution. All of his book titles are so creative. He was a multi-talented person. He was a poet, lyricist, actor and author. Vishwambara was his master piece. For that he won the famous Gnana Peet award.

43. Telangana's literature

Telangana's literature was very ancient

It started from the time of Shathavahana

Then, Gatha Saptasati was a famous text

It was written in Pakriti language by Hala

The poems in it were about love and joy

These were narrated by an unmarried girl

She wanted to see a boy with feeling of coy

All the poems were about lust and love feel

Like Gatha Saptassti, There were plenty

Gunadya's Brihatkata, Vastayana's Kamasutra

Kuthuhala wrote Parinayam of Leelavathi

They were all about love and life's propaganda

Meaning:

Telangana literature is very old. It started from the time of Shathavahana. Gatha Saptasati was the famous text, which was written in Pakriti language by Hala. The book was about love and joy. Like this, there were Gunadya's Brihatkata, Vastyana's Kamasutra were famous texts.

44. South Kumbhamela

Medaram's fair is Telangana's Kumbha Mela
It is the biggest one in the continent, Asia
Its importance was recognized by UNESCO
So, Medaram's history, everyone has to know
Padigidderaju married the daughter of Medaraju
Sammakka was her name, she's a sacred woman
Due to drought, taxes weren't paid by Padigidderaju
So, the king, Prathaparudra invaded their domain
Sammakka and her children fought as an animal
Army killed Jampanna, Saralamma, her children
Later, she had disappeared at the parrots' hill
At the hill, the tribal found turmeric and saffron

Meaning:

Medaram fair is the largest one in Asia after Kumbhamela. So it is treated as south's Kumbhamela. Even UNESCO recognised its importance. There was a story behind it. Sammakka and Sarakka, the two brave women fought for their tribal kingdom. In the wasr, Sammakka was disappeared in the forest at a hill. Now at that place, the fair is being taken place.

45. The Deccan Plateau

• 45 •

Telangana is on the Deccan Plateau

It has many brilliant and classic arts

Ramalingeswara temple is nouveau

It stands as a testimony of Kakitayas

The temple thrills its panoramic view

The visitors will admire its architecture

Telanganites should not try to eschew

It is a true symbol of Telangana culture

The temple got its name on the sculptor

So, everyone calls it as Ramappa temple

Here, people adore the god, Rudreshwar

It is only the temple of period, medieval

Meaning:

Telangana is on the Deccan Plateau. The plateau is famous for many classical arts. The Kakatiyan architecture is very famous on it. Ramappa temple is one such example.

46. Thousand Pillar Temple

Telangana's pride is Thousand Pillar Temple

It is popular pilgrimage center to be visited

You are amazed to see the construction style

The deities, Vishnu, Shiva and Sun are adored

The architecture of the temple is star shaped

All of the thousand pillars were grandly carved

You'll know the expertise of Kakitayan period

In Center, huge monolith blacksalt Nandi is stood

The king, Rudradeva constructed this temple

Later, it was partly damaged during Tuglaq's rule

It is a belief that the faiths come true of all

So, everyone loves to visit the famous temple

Meaning:

Telangana's other pride is Thousand Pillar Temple. It is located in the heart of Warangal city. Everyone is amazed to look the architecture style of it. Lod Vishnu, Shiva and the sun are worshipped in it. All thousand pillars are carved grandly. The king, Rudradeva constructed the temple.

47. Divine Basara

Basara is a divine place in district, Nirmal
Gnana Saraswathi is the deity in the temple
The temple is situated on the bank of Godavari
The word, Basara came from Vyasa Maharshi
Vyasa had spent here after Kurukshetra war
He used to perform his puja at Godavari River
Thus, the place Vasar had turned into Basar
The king, Birbala had built the temple here
Saraswathi, Lakshmi and Kali are holy Trinity
Every year, the people celebrate Mahashivarathri
The children come here before formal education
For Akshara Abhyasam, it is an ideal destination

Meaning:

Basara is the divine place in Telangana. It is located in Nirmal district. Gnana Saraswathi is the deity in the temple. Basara came from Vyasa Maharshi. Vyasa spent here after Kurukshetra war. There are many stories behind it.

48. The wooden toys

Nirmal is famous for wooden toys
It has the glorious history of years
You can see amazing epic paintings
The place is also well-known for forts
Years back, cannons were sold here
Nizam used to buy them for the war
Nimma Naidu was a ruler of Nirmal
Later, the place was called as Nirmal
Visitors won't return without buying
The toys and paintings are appealing
For artisans, buying is so encouraging
All of them are living on this making
Meaning:
Nirmal is famous for wooden toys. The place has a glorious history. You can see the distinct epic paintings here. The city is also famous for forts. It is said that Nijam bought cannons for the war.

49. Telangana's Ooty

Ananthagiri Hills is a tourist place

Plan it, it will be a wonderful trip

The beauty isn't lesser than Ooty's

It can open your eyes and wake up

Your surreal dreams come true here

The spiral roads can thrill you more

You come to know, Musi isn't a drain

It's god Padmanabhaswami's domain

The spot is best for the sport, trekking

Its beauty oozes beautifully stunning

For the poor, it's a place for honeymoon

Lovers here develop their interaction

Meaning:

Ananthagiri is considered as Telangana's Ooty. It is serene place in Telangana. The river Musi was born in the place. It is the best tourist spot for the people who can't afford to go to long places.

50. Telangana Thirupathi

Manyamkonda is the poor's Thirupathi
Venkateshwara here is Swayambumurthi
Once many saints meditated on the hill
So it is considered as the place of spiritual
The temple was built in a cave on the hill
If you visit it, you definitely will feel thrill
The fair is held on Magha full moon day
Piligrims from many states come and stay
The natural un-dig Koneru is a lovely site
Few things are resembled to Tirumala
Like seven hills, seven gates were built
Manyamkonda recalls Thirumalakonda

Meaning:

Manyamkonda is considered as Telangana Thirupathi. There are many similarities with Thirupathi. Like seven hills in Thirupathi, there are seven gates. Lord, Venkateshwara is Swayambumurthi. Undug Koneru is the special attraction to this place.

51. The state festival

Bonalu is Telangana's state festival
In Telugu, Bonam literally means meal
Women cook it with rice and jaggery
Later they offer it to the deity Kali
Plague disease broke out in the past
The disease took the lives of thousand
The military prayed for Kali in MP state
Plague gradually halted and stopped
In Ashadam, Bonalu begins at Golkonda
Kali is adored in Yellamma, Pochamma
Pothuraju dance is the special attraction
Meat feast for relatives is real celebration

Meaning:

Bonalu is Telangana's state festival. Bonam means meal. The meal is cooked in a pot and offered to Kali for fulfiling their desires. This is celebrated grandly during the month of Ashada. The people enjoy the festival very much. It is a good practice worshipping the different godesses.

52. Sacred Ramzan

Ramzan falls in ninth month of Islamic
Muslims do fast from dawn to dusk
Pre-dawn meal is referred as Suhur
The feast in the night is called as Ifthar
Sawab of fasting is doubled in Ramzan
Some sinful things, they should refrain
The Quran is the guidance for mankind
It teaches, "Everyone should be disciplined"
The Islam is the practice of monotheism
It says to do prayer, fasting, alms, and pilgrim
It tells, good deeds bring them rewards
And it spreads too many good practices

Meaning:

Ramzan falls in the ninth of month of Islamic calendar. Muslims are on the fast during this from early morning to night. Morning meal is called as Suhur and evening meal is called as Ifthar. During this, the people lead very sacred life by doing alms to the poor.

53. Nagoba-traditional fair

Nagoba is tribal's ten day festival

The Gonds clean temple in old pitchers

The Gonds' king does a long ritual

It is behting, "Introducing brides"

A year later, brides get eligibility

Then they pray for deity, Janubai

With grains, food is prepared freshly

It's a form of thanksgiving to Janubai

Later, they perform Gusadi dance

It's main attraction to the fair, Nagoba

Every event has a special purpose

They continue Mahapuja, it is Persa

Meaning:

Nagoba is the second largest fair in Telangana. It is the tribals festival, celebrated for ten days. It is celebrated according to their customs. They worship the goddess, Janubai. They perform Gusadi dance during the fair.

54. Charming Charminar

Telangana means Hyderabad
Hyderabad means the Charminar
The Charminar is very privileged
Privileged live near the Charminar
It's a cultural signature monument
It's built to eradicate Plague disease
Visitors won't go without seeing it
It'll be a lifelong memory to visitors
For women, the place is a paradise
They will get all emporium items
The history is connected to lives
It became a part of people's hearts

Meaning:

The Charminar is privileged place to Hyderabad and Telangana. Everyone craves to visit the Charminar when they come to Hyderabad. It is the best cultural monument. For emporium items, the place is the best for women. It was built by Muhammad Kuli Kudub Shaw to eradicate Plague disease.

55. Yummy Cuisines

Telangana cuisines are very yummy
The first place goes to spicy biryani
For healthy tiffin, there's Sarvapindi
For alcohol lovers, there's Boti curry
For snacks, people make Malidalu
On Pongal, they prepare Sakinalu
For crispy sweet, they eat Garijalu
On Ugadi, they enjoy having Polelu
On wedding, it is Kurbhani Mita
For vegetarians, there's Puntikura
For relatives, it is Natukodi kura
For strength, there is soup of paya

Meaning:

Telangana cuisines are very tasty. Hyderabad biryani takes the first place. Sakinalu, Garjelu, Polelu and many others are very tasty. After seperation of Telangana, the cuines have got good prominence.

56. Secular State

Telangana is a true secular state
The culture is blend of all religions
For each religion, it's a monument
Every village has temples, churches
Medak church is Telangana's pride
In Asia, it is the most visited place
After Vatican church, it's considered
At a time five thousand offer prayers
The cathedral was built by Posnett
Thousands of labourers worked for it
The construction is in Gothic style
During drought, it served the people
Meaning:
Telangana is the best secular state in India. Hyderbad is Mini India. One can see all castes and creeds, regions and religions are found in Hyderabad. Apart from this, it is famous for churches, mosques and temples. Medak church is the biggest one in the Asia.

57. Jain Shrine in Telangana

Kolanupaka is Jain Shrine in Telangana

It has idols of Mahaveer, Neminath, Rishabha

The temple is two thousand years old

For Jains, the temple is a very sacred abode

The temple is popular for its architecture

The aura of it, make you feel conjecture

The people are irritated with traffic in cities

For peaceful environment it is the best place

The temple is a true replica of secularism

Irrespective of religion, people will come

From a regular busy life, you may feel boredom

Visit the place to know the history of Jainism

Meaning:

Kulpakji also Kolanupaka Temple is a 2,000 year-old Jain temple at the village of Kolanupaka in Aler City, Yadadri district, Telangana, India. The temple houses three idols: one each of Lord Rishabhanatha, Lord Neminatha, and Lord Mahavira

58. VISA god

You mightn't listen about VISA god
There are many gods for many religions
There is a god for the unemployed
That god is in Chilkur, it is lord Balaji's
The temple is on the bank of Osman Sagar
For spirituality, the temple is an epicentre
If the people come to the village, Chilkur,
their desire will definitely be fulfilled in a year
Here everyone has to stand in a queue
The temple does not think of its revenue
Like other temples, you will not see hundi
And the priests does not crave for money

Meaning:

Chilkur Balaji Temple, popularly known as "Visa Balaji Temple", is an ancient Hindu temple of Lord Balaji on the banks of Osman Sagar in Rangareddy District. It is one of the oldest temples in Hyderabad Dist earlier now in Rangareddy Dist. built during the time of Madanna and Akkanna, the uncles of Bhakta Ramadas

59. The Nightingale

Sarojini Naidu was born in Telangana

She is called as the nightingale of India

Her poems reflected the culture of Telangana

Her activism made her first governor of India

She studied in the University of Cambridge

Her statesmanship was very privilege

Sarojini Naidu was also an active suffrage

For women, even today she is an image

The theme of writings were about patriotism

She contributed to the country in many ways

As a poet and leader, she tried to transform

A woman in those days showed her expertise

Meaning:

Sarojini Naidu was an Indian political activist and poet. A proponent of civil rights, women's emancipation, and anti-imperialistic ideas, she was an important figure in India's struggle for independence from colonial rule.

60. The powerful woman

Arutla Kamaladevi was a woman activist
She is a model of women empowerment
She participated in Telangana movement
To jail, Kamaladevi was many times sent
Arutla was the first woman MLA of Telangana
She won as MLA from Bhuvanagiri and Aler
She led the farmers' movement of Telangana
She inspired the followers of Communist Party
Arutla's personal life inspires so many women
Even after the marriage, she studied and worked
She held pen and to change the society, held gun
As a wife, activist and leader her role is fulfilled

Meaning:

Arutla Kamala Devi was a prominent figure and activist of the Telangana Armed Rebellion. She along with her partner Arutla Ramachandra Reddy were pioneers and led the movement based in the Aleru region of Nalgonda.

61. The hidden place of Telangana

Telangana is a state for amazing scenery

There are many hidden beautiful places

If you explore, the nature shows its beauty

Kunthala waterfalls is one of such places

The waterfall is at inhabitation of Gonds

The Water falls from the highest point

Visitors are thrilled to look its beauties

It sounds like a musician's instrument

The word, Kunthala came from Shakunthala

Shakunthala was the wife of Dushyantha

Once she used to take bath in this waterfall

Mahashivarathri is here the grand festival

Meaning:

Kuntala Waterfall is a waterfall in the indian state of Telangana, located on Kadam river in Neradigonda mandal of Adilabad district. It is the highest waterfall in the state with a height of fifty meters. These waterfalls are in the dense forests inhabited by the Gonds. Kunta in Gondi and Telugu means pond.

62. Bhuvanagiri Fort

The biggest monolith hill is in Telangana
Its massive structure is the country's pride
There the fort was built by Vikramaditya
It's Tribhuvanagiri, Bhuvanagiri now called
The fort had belonged to Chalukyan Period
Even today it is the famous heritage center
See, you'll feel as if you were in a fairy land,
when you travel beside the town, Bhongir
It is the best panoramic view on the region
The Fort has the oldest temple of Hanuman
Many adventurers come here for trekking
While ascending, they feel very thrilling

Meaning:

The Bhongir fort adorns the place from the time it was built in 10th century. Bhongir Fort was built on an isolated monolithic rock by the Western Chalukya ruler Tribhuvanamalla Vikramaditya IV in the year 1076 and was thus named after him as Tribhuvanagiri, later it was called as Bhuvanagiri. Some of the inscriptions found in the fort were in Kannada and Telugu language highlighting the lifestyle of the people of that era.

63. Oggu Katha

Oggu Katha is a traditional folklore
In Telangana, Oggu is very popular
It is originated from Kuruma caste
The performers sing, dance, and narrate
It is narrating stories of hindu gods
Midde Ramulu is so famous for this
Chukka Sathaiah took it to abroad
These Two made Telangana proud
Instruments used are Dolu, Thalam
Exciting thing is Shiva's Damarukam
The art has exciting dramatization
It has a lot of scope for improvisation

Meaning:

Oggu Katha is a beautiful folklore of Telangana. Midde Ramulu and Chukka Sathaiah brought fame to this. It is the combination of singing, dancing, and narrating which is very difficult to perform.

64. The rising sun

I walk daily in the morning
My path is towards a tank
There, I see the sun shining
I'm awestruck, my soul sank
The sun rays kissing the water
Water is thrilled and it flowed
The silent ducks moved further
The sight made me unmoved
The sun not only awakes people
-but also elicits their hidden soul
The happiness is imprinted on
-the heart and makes day shine

Meaning:

Everyday I go for a walk in the morning towards a tank. There I see the beautiful rising sun. He fills hope and positivity in the people. Even the water feel thrilled when he arrives. The inactive birds and animals dance at once. When anyone sees the beauty, the whole day is filled with full of positivity.

65. Pembarthi- An artistic place

Pembarthi is famous for art crafts
The engravings are of ancient days
The history of it is very exquisite
Here it was used, Kakitayan style of art
Chariots and statues are prepared
They look like works of the ancient
Everywhere their skill is appreciated
Pembarthi is Telangana's artefact
Ancient art of Pembarthi is survived
The art is modified but it is revived
Now the art is multi religions' blend
Finally Pembarthi is the state's pride

Meaning:

Pembarthi is village famous for its metal handicrafts and brass works. Lots of people are skilled in the making of Statues,awards and presentations. Pembarthi Brassware, over the years has captured the essential nuances of both Hindu and Muslim influences, which has seamlessly blended into both cultures. The craft form has received the prestigious Geographical Indication, which is indeed an honour for the craft.

66. Cheryala- Nakashi art

Cheryala is associated with Nakashi art
The paintings reflect Telangana culture
Each painting is in a narrative format
The paintings are Telangana's treasure
The paintings are painted on Khadi cloth
The painters mostly use primary colours
For background, red hue is the strength
The paintings reflect the local professions
Vishnu, Shiva and Krishna are painted
Themes of Mahabharatha are attracted
You do not have to read Garudapunam
Cheryala arts depict epics' compendium

Meaning:

The scroll paintings are traditionally painted on a khadi cloth after the fabric is processed with sawdust, tamarind-seed paste, rice starch, white mud and tirumani, or tree gum. The canvas is allowed to dry and the priming process is repeated once, after which it is ready to use once dry.

67. Komuravelli Mallanna

Komuravelli is a famous temple in Telangana
The deity in the temple is lord Mallikarjuna
Mallikarjuna is an incarnation of Lord Shiva
The Maharashtrians call the deity as Khanoba
Once Kumaraswami meditated at Komuravelli
Hence, the village name became Komuravelli
The temple's fair is renowned all over country
The fair starts on Sankranti and ends on Ugadi
Long back, the deity is made with soil of anthill
Still the deity looks beautiful and ceremonial
The sacred place is flourished as it is historical
It is the best place to fulfil the desires of people

Meaning:

Mallanna along with his consorts Golla Kethamma, Goddess Ganga and Medalamma, Goddess Parvati are at the main temple. The Oggu Katha singers sing the tale of Mallanna here. Devotees offer prayers to Mallanna with the help of Oggu Pujaris who draw a rangoli called as Patnam (A form of offering prayers to Lord) in front of Lord Mallanna inside temple and also in temple's verandah.

68. Telangana heaven

Pakhala is the second purest lake in the country
Visiting Pakhala is a part of exploring wildlife
You will be thrilled to see the forest's beauty
This is a part of unforgettable experiences in life
Pakhala was dug during the eleventh century
Water of it is used for drinking and irrigation
This is the country's biggest crocodiles' sanctuary
To its beauty the state govt arranged zip lane
The Pakhala Lake is like Telangana's paradise
You listen to songs of the birds and cries of animals
The lake is surrounded by the beautiful hills
To savour the beauty of nature one definitely visits

Meaning:

Pakhal Lake is an artificial lake situated in the Pakhal sanctuary close to Warangal City in Telangana. Believed to have been constructed in 1213 A.D by order of the Kakatiya King Ganapathidev, the lake encompasses an area of 30 sq km. Set around the lake is the Pakhal Wildlife Sanctuary spread over an area of 900 sq km.

69. Food- Form of lord Brahma

Lord Brahma creates human beings
Human beings produce food for existence
Existence becomes tougher without food
Food is the primary need to be happy
Happiness comes from the comforts
The one and only comfort is eating
Eating food is not a part of daily chores
It is experiencing for the satisfaction
The satisfaction is essential for anyone
One should be happy with what they've
Everybody has the source of getting food
So food is treated as other form of Brahma

Meaning:

Food is the other form of Brahma. For human existence, it is the most essential thing. Lord Brahma made human beings and the human beings live eating food. Happiness mainly comes from food. So one has to respect food.

70. Modi- No jeopardy

Jeopardy itself is afraid of Modi
Modi faces anything and anybody
The pandemic is controlled by Modi
Modi is the best buddy of everybody
He is the affectionate son of India
He made India, the country of utopia
His rule to the people is euphoria
Chay wallah was Modi's nostalgia
The country's being is brought back
by him which was once drawback
Enemies are worried of counterattack
Lastly the country is safe in his look

Meaning:

There is no worry to the country while Modi is ruling the country. His leadership is found in many situations. During the pandemic his bravery is seen. Within less time, he changed India in many aspects. So people call him as the affectionate son of India.

71. Brave Bhagath

Bhagath Singh was a radical hero

Inquilab Zindabad is only his motto

He killed Saunders, who killed Rai

The incident made the British annoy

Singh sacrificed his life for India

His valour, courage created phobia

So the British tried curb his mania

But the mania made them insomnia

Singh's journey from an editor to

a freedom fighter couldn't continue

He gave up everything for the country

Thus he became youngsters' celebrity

Meaning:

Bhagat Singh was a charismatic Indian revolutionary who participated in the murder of a junior British police officer and an Indian head constable in mistaken retaliation for the death of an Indian nationalist. His sacrifice filled the patriotism in the Indians.

72. The man of millennium

Abdul Kalam is the man of millennium

Kalam is another source of empiricism

He tells the children to fulfil their dream

Thus he became replica of humanism

Abdul Kalam is walking encyclopedia

From a paper boy to President of India,

From a scientist to the head of DRDO,

Kalam grew and work was only his motto

It was just listening in the moral stories

about a man with morals and values

Abdul Kalam is one of the examples

in leading simple life with noble principles

Meaning:

Avul Pakir Jainulabdeen Abdul Kalam was an Indian aerospace scientist who served as the 11th president of India from 2002 to 2007. He was born and raised in Rameswaram, Tamil Nadu and studied physics and aerospace engineering. He is the walking encyclopaedia. He is the best example for following morals and ethics.

73. UNO-A peace maker

The UNO develops the relations
Its main aim is to prevent wars
It also protects human rights
Thus it builds the confidence
The UNO has six principal organs
They work for humans' progess
Its officials won many Nobel prizes
It has become symbol for peace
Every year, it has a special theme
Now, it's "Recovering the system"
We know, Covid-19's vandalism
It wants the pandemic's doom

Meaning:

The United Nations is an international organization founded in 1945 after the Second World War by 51 countries committed to maintaining international peace and security, developing friendly relations among nations and promoting social progress, better living standards and human rights.

74. Abul Kalam Azad

Abul Kalam Azad was a great thinker

He was an intellectual freedom fighter

To khilafath movement, he was a leader

To the poor people, he was a pathfinder

His interest in the education is amazing

His fluency in languages is outstanding

The education is enlightenment of soul

The soul becomes liberal and universal

He struggled a lot for Indian Independence

His broad political views helped the Indians

Now he's the role model to Muslim Minorities

His birthday is celebrated with the reverence

Meaning:

Abul Kalam Azad, original name Abul Kalam Ghulam Muhiyuddin, also called Maulana Abul Kalam Azad or Maulana Azad, born November 11, 1888, Mecca, now in Saudi Arabia, died on February 22, 1958, New Delhi, India, Islamic theologian who was one of the leaders of the Indian independence movement against British rule. He was the first education minister. On his birth, we celebrate Minorities Day on November 11th every year.

75. A beautiful tourist spot

Laknavaram is a beautiful tourist spot

To Telangana, it is the best heritage site

It is one of the eco-friendly places

It will remain memory to the tourists

The lake was dug by Kakatiya dynasty

You can see the spectacular water body

It is located in Jayashankar Bhupalapally

Laknavaram Lake is pride to geography

Special attraction here is hanging bridge

To the tourists, it is a special advantage

To Telangana State, the lake is privilege

You will get happiness of overvoltage

Meaning:

The lake was built by the rulers of the Kakatiya dynasty in 13th Century A.D. Explore the massive Laknavaram Lake, a spectacular waterbody located in the Jayshankar-Bhupalpally district of Telangana. This breath takingly beautiful lake is an amazing and popular tourist spot in Telangana. The lake is simply an exceptional thing of beauty. It is well-known for its wonderful hanging bridge, considered one-of-its-kind in the state.

76. The best tourist destination

Palair Lake is the best tourist destination
The lake is an important tourist attraction
For the tourists is a very good recreation
Water in it is useful during kharif season
It is also a major source for drinking water
It is a balancing reservoir for Lal Bahadur,
which is a left canal for Nagarjuna Sagar
It covers the area of thousands of hectars
The lake always reveals its natural beauty
The tourists are fascinated wonderfully
It is the best location for cinematography
If you visit the place, you will get serenity

Meaning:

Palair Lake is a man made lake and a major source of freshwater in the Khammam district of Telangana, India. It is located at the Palair village in Kusumanchi mandal of the district and is about 30 kilometers away from the district headquarters of Khammam.

77. A mass leader

CM. KCR is the masses' leader
KCR is an abled administrator
He has excellent political career
In India, he's the best chief minister
His strength is his grip on language
He knows the languages' usage
Eloquent speech is his advantage
With it, people immediately change
CM. KCR knows rebuttal information
He always puts his ideas in execution
Today, he is an example of statesman
KCR is Telangana's father of nation

Meaning:

C.M KCR is the real mass leader and abled administrator. His strength is the grip on the language and able to interact with masses. He comes with the facts and figures which amaze the people. All his words are put into actions. He made it impossible possible that is achieving Telangana.

78. Singa Samudram waterfall

Near our village, a waterfall is located
Its hidden beauty has been unveiled
Our local people are so much excited
Nobody knows, before it is explored
Singa Samudram waterfall, it is called
Kakatiyan Vassal King constructed
It belonged to Prathaparudra's period
All these days, this was unspecified
Watch! You feel as if you're in abroad
With its beauty, you will be amazed
And your eyes will never be closed
The image is permanently recorded

Meaning:

Singa Samudram was built by Singama raju, the vassal king of Kakatiya kingdom. On his name it is being called as Singa Samudram. If you visit the spot, you feel like as if you were in foreign.

79. The tributary of the Godavari

Manair is the tributary of the Godavari
Beautiful locations are at the tributary
Of these, higher Manair dam goes firstly
In Telangana State, it is the best scenery
Higher Manair Dam was built at Narmala
It is considered as Telangana's Nayagara
as it is one of the widest barrages in India
It was constructed during Nizam's era
For beautiful places you need not to longer
You will find plenty many places closer
The nature is waiting to show its splendour
Higher Manair will definitely be a wonder

Meaning:

Manair is the tributary of river Godavari. There are many beautiful locations beside it. Higher Manair Dam is one of such that. You will remember Nayagara waterfalls after seeing it.

80. Smart Staff

Our Principal is pretty personality
Our coordinator is school operator
Our PGT Telugu's voice is like cuckoo
Our TGT Telugu is the silent guru
Our TGT Hindi's class is extraordinary
Our PGT Urdu's words are like Sadhu
Our TGT Urdu is calm, doesn't argue
Our TGT English is stylish, unselfish
Our TGT Maths is a man of goodness
Our TGT Maths is a woman of pious
Our TGT Science's quality is tolerance
Our PGT Physics is very spontaneous
Our PGT Biology has a good ideology
Our TGT Social is very professional
Our Art Teacher has very good heart
Our Nurse Teacher won't compromise
Our PET can wonderfully write poetry

Meaning:

The above poem depicts the good personality of my colleagues in TMRS Jangaon-Boys-1.

81. Charming Children

We should keep children happy
-because their souls are pretty
They make the premises noisy
Their parents beat them badly
Our stress is reduced by them
They retain our lives with charm
They fill happiness in the vacuum
So give them complete freedom
They will crave for simple things
They may be chocolates or toys
Provide them, knowing the needs
Otherwise they will make mess
Childhood is the life's best part
When you grow, it will be past
The part has to be happily spent
-because, "Our life is very short"

Meaning:

We should keep the children happy as they are innocent beings. They make noise but we do not irritate at them. The parents' worries disappear when they look their children. So give them some freedom as they are innocent souls.

82. Nampally Hill

A temple is nestled on a small hillock

The deity in it made of the oldest rock

To reach the place, it has the stairs' track

There you will see the snake of gigantic

The temple is located in Vemulawada

It is widely known as Nampally Gutta

The deity is the lord, Laxminarasimha

The place is a pride to State Telangana

The biggest snake was built grandly

You can enter through the snake's belly

You are thrilled to look at strange deity

It depicts the god killing the demon badly

Meaning:

An ancient temple is located on the hillock of Nampally which is near to Vemulawada. The most interesting thing on the hill is the biggest snake is built. You can go through the snake and experience amazingly. In the snake's belly, you will find Lord Laxmi Narasimha.

83. Falknuma Palace

• 83 •

Viqar-ul-Umra was Hyderabad's minister
The buildings in Europe astonished Viqar
Thus Falknuma Palace was built by him
Mirrors of the sky is the palace's other name
It is in the form of Venetian architecture
The palace has grand and brilliant furniture
All the rooms are with beautiful structure
You will also find the Quran's scripture
In Telangana, it is the best heritage site
As the costly hotel, this will highlight
At least one should stay for a fortnight
Then only you know the greatness of it

Meaning:

It was built by Nawab Sir Viqar-ul-Umra, Prime Minister of Hyderabad and the uncle & brother-in-law of the sixth Nizam. Falak-numa means "Like the Sky" or "Mirror of Sky" in Urdu. It is as grand and spectacular as the Buckingham Palace in London. Brilliant in design and luxurious in décor, the palace stands tall commanding an awe of its being a rare architecture. Only five kms away from the Charminar, Falaknuma Palace is a must visit.

84. The Golkonda

• 84 •

Golkonda was the capital of Qutub Shahis
It is undeniably treasure of Telanganites
Golkonda once was famous for diamonds
Kohinur diamond was found in the hills
Once the fort was called as Golla Konda
It was built by the dynasty of Kakatiya
It was protected during rule of Rani Rudrama
The fort was strengthened by Prathaparudra
Nizam nawabs ruled the state, living in it
The fort was evidence for people's poignant
Later people got freedom from the fort
Now, the national flag is hoisted in the fort

Meaning:

It was originally a mud fort under the reign of Rajah of Warangal. Later it was fortified between 14th and 17th centuries by the Bahmani Sultans and then the ruling Qutub Shahi dynasty. Golconda was the principal capital of the Qutub Shahi kings.

85. The Dam- State's esteem

Nagarjuna Sagar Dam is state's esteem
This is the world's largest masonry dam
One'll clearly see the engineers' wisdom
It's also another pretty place for tourism
It's built during India's first five year plan
With this, barren lands turned into green
Boating experience will remain in brain
The picturesque will caught your attention
You'll find a oldest museum on the island
The museum is set up in serene greenwood
There, the historic artefacts are preserved
After the visit, you feel very much satisfied

Meaning:

Nagarjuna Sagar Dam is a masonry dam across the Krishna River at Nagarjuna Sagar which straddles the border between Nalgonda district in Telangana and Guntur district in Andhra Pradesh. World's largest masonry dam protected with 26 gates measuring 124.663m in height , Nagarjunasagar Dam located in Nalgonda District is built across River Krishna. The dam has a storage capacity of nearly 11,472 million cubic meters with an irrigation capacity for 9.81 lac acres of land.

86. Famous for fairs

Telangana State is very famous for fairs
Peddagattu Lingamathula is one of them
Shiva, Choudamma are offered prayers
It's the second biggest fair after Medaram
Though it is the festival of Yadava castes,
the people from many states come here
The fair's celebrated grandly for five days,
praying to look after them in ecosphere
Lingas are usually offered Veg-Prasadam
Here Nonveg-Prasadam is shown to Lingam
Shiva's sister, Choudamma is also adored
Peddagattu fair is crowded but very sacred

Meaning:

Peddagattu or Gollagattu Jathara is the festival done in the name of Lord Lingamanthulu Swamy and Goddess Choudamma every two years. The presiding deities, Sri Lingamanthula Swamy, believed an Incarnation of Lord Shiva, and his sister – Choudamma, are offered various pujas during the five-day fete.

87. Aadi Shakthi

Aadi Shakthi is born from Omkara
She created Brahma, Vishnu, and Shiva
Later Saraswathi, Laxmi, Parvathi
Together of these three, it is Kali
Devotees' dear deity is Maisamma
Her form is solemn but blesses them
The deity is formed under the neem
Looking her in the anthill is enigma!
The temple is in the village of Amangal
It was built during Nijam Nawab's rule
It's developed by Nalavath personnel
Now, it was beautiful place of spiritual
Meaning:
Aadi Shakthi is born from Omkara. She created Brahma, Vishnu, and Shiva. Later Saraswathi, Laxmi, Parvathi. Together of these three, it is Kali.

88. Kalabhairava

Kalabhairava Temple is in Kamareddy
It is only temple in southern country
Karthika astami is celebrated grandly
The day is treated as swamy's jayanthi
Kalabhairava is savior of Kasikshetra
He is Lord Shiva's dear son of mind
He even had fought with Lord Brahma
After Kasikshetra it is second sacred
Black magic victims visit the temple
They will stay here for their survival
People's problems might be anything
All obstacles will be solved by offering

Meaning:

Kalabhairava Temple is in Kamareddy. It is only temple in southern country. Karthika astami is celebrated grandly. The day is treated as swamy's jayanthi

89. The qualities of Telanganites

Strife is the quality of Telanganites
Peace is imbibed from the ancestors
Helping the needy is in their prowess
They are so frank, but not spurious
They agitate with the nonviolence
They always fight with the braveness
Their dialect style is nice, fabulous
In life, they live with audaciousness
They preach to come out of indoors
Onerous things are as easy as ABCs
They don't feel bad for simple things
Their lifestyle is inspiration to others

Meaning:

Telangana has multi-qualities. Strife, nonviolence, braveness are some of them. The people of the state are also simple but great.

90. Men-the companions

Problems of the men are hidden
In life, they do not have salvation
They always forget their position,
remain as companion to women
This state is not only in one nation
It is even in Oman, Japan, Sudan
At least on "Men's day occasion"
know the contributions of the men
As a father, friend and any relation,
the men always fulfil that position
So the man is human, not machine
But the men always will be the men

Meaning:

Problems of the men are hidden. No one notices their problems. It is not only pertained to India but to many countries.

91. Home to many

Home to the arts is Telangana
Stage to the songs is Telangana
Junction to dharnas is our state
Place to the strives is our state
Heart to braveness is our land
Land to myriad cultures of old
Daring is in the people's fist
Success will only be their thirst
Sacrifice for the land is quality
Adventure is only their identity
For friendship they do anything
So the land is always in leading

Meaning:

Telangana is home to arts, songs, dharnas, agitations and cultures. The state's gives residence for anyone and anything.

92. Sacred Telangana

Telangana is the land of sacred rivers

The Godavari is feeding state's lands

The Krishna's water removes dryness

The Manjeera is the point of projects

Singareni coal mine is pure, pristine

NTPC in India is in well-known position

Waterfalls' and hills' beauty is hidden

Art on state's temples is phenomenon

Kagaz Nagar paper mill was the oldest

Nizam Sugars factory was the largest

Kohinur is diamond of heavier carat

All these are ornaments to the state

Meaning:

Telangana is sacred place as it has pure rivers. It is said that the civilizations are developed on the river banks. Godavari, Krishna rivers make the state unique.

93. The grand history

The history of Telangana is grand
In the market, diamonds were sold
Signs of the barbarians were found
Asmaka Janapda is part of the land
Once it was said that Telangana,
-our state came from Kondanna
He was one of disciples of Bhudda
Kondapur is township of Bhudda
Later state became heritage center
And grew to state of super power
Faced many problems with center
Finally Telangana stood as winner

Meaning:

The history of Telangana is grand. Once the diamonds and gems were sold in the market as if they were vegetables. The greatest people made the state glorious.

94. TMREIS- A symbol of success

TMREIS focuses on the success
It fulfils the needs of the students
Teaching, here is with examples
Thus it changes the students' lives
Its schools are set up in the nature
The buildings have good furniture
It has a nice curriculum structure
It is famous for classroom culture
The food and water are hygienic
So the students are enthusiastic
It's the best society for academic
In TMREIS, everything is systematic

Meaning:

TMREIS is symbol of success. It is established by the state government to reach out the best education to the poorest of the poor students. All the schools have good facilities.

95. The slavish life

The slavish life has to end
Power should be in hand
of the underprivileged
This message has to passed
We should try to fill the light
as their life is the darkest
Now, it is the time to unite
and rule with more effort
The souls of great leaders
have to appease with this
Make all the communities
develop, then they're joyous

Meaning:

The slavish life has to end. Power should be in hand of everyone. When that dream is fulfilled, the national leaders' dream will be fulfilled.

96. Listening is an art

Who is the great person?
One who is in position?
Or who has lot of money?
Or who has full of mighty?
No, the great person is one
who listens with attention,
irrespective of the position
everyone including veteran
Listening is a good soft skill
Without knowing this, all
react without reciprocating
Everyone needs skill of listening

Meaning:

Listening is an art. First one should learn to listen not to speak. It is lacking even with the great people now a days. They always react without listening to the people

97. Study well

Why don't you study well?
Don't you know the level
of your parents' potential?
Study well, life will be beautiful
If you are not told, it's okay
You don't listen even we say
No study, no life, don't delay
When do you? If it isn't today
Try to change your destiny
Make your parents happy
Your life always shouldn't be
like the clothes which are dirty

Meaning:

Education is the best weapon to change ourselves but people are neglecting. We give priority to unimportant things without giving priority to education.

98. The poor

Sometimes I feel very sad
I cry at their life of devoid
They have two acres of land
It'll be one after they divide
Their hard work feed the kids
But the kids are senseless
They don't listen to classes
They don't see the success
If you don't study, no life
If you study you will be safe
And you will get good wife
Life long, you will get relief

Meaning:

Sometimes I feel the pathetic condition of the poor. I feel that the poor should not become poorer. Only education make them rich.

99. Craving communities

Gouds should rise to go into the space

Potters should become the politicians

Weavers can become worldwide famous

Carpenters should be the kingmakers

SCs should administer their states

STs should come out of the forests

Mudirajs should become the managers

Gangaputras can become govt employees

Chakalis should be the champions

Yadavas' yearning can become "yes"

Artists should go to the law houses

In Telangana all communities can rise

Meaning:

All the underprivileged sections would become politicians, business men, professionals. Then only Ambedkar's dream will be fulfilled.

100. My life in brief

I was born into a poor family
I did part time jobs for my study
My parents studied up to degree
I didn't study more due to no money
But my father impacted me morally
Society's negligence made me feel guilty
Then I decided to transform totally
My father's demise affected me badly
Then I again have chosen to study
With that, I became govt employee
Later I started writing books greatly
Finally I became a writer successfully

Meaning:

The poem depicts my life in brief. My self motivation made me a writer and teacher. My life taught me good lessons than my study.

101. Our Constitution

Our constitution is called as supreme law of India
The preamble starts with we, the people of India
The colonial India turned into the Republic India
Justice, liberty, equality are the qualities of India
Dr. Ambedkar is the father of Indian constitution
The committee drafted it with a great devotion
In the world, it is the biggest written constitution
Constitution is drafted for the Indians' integration
The acts were borrowed from the different nations
It was based on the people's needs and necessities
The constitution is the model for so many nations
The administration with it will be smooth process

Meaning:

Indian constitution is the largest written constitution in the world. It was drafted by Ambedkar and his team. It basically tells fraternity, secularism, freedom and equality.

102. Our Great History

The history of India is ancient
Telangana's history is so great
Fighting is Telanganites' spirit
Achieve what they exactly want
Nonviolence is the state's quality
It is inspired by Indian history
India got its freedom healthily
The reason is Gandhi's ideology
Nonviolence solves many hurdles
Telangana solved its struggles
It is inspiration to other nations
India is model to peaceful agitations

Meaning:

The poem tells that the history of Telangana is so great. Fighting is our spirit and nonviolence is our quality.

103. Active Soul

Hidden strength has to come out
The active soul should try to fight
Fighting spirit is always benevolent
It makes the people's lives bright
Silent souls cause pain to society
If pain remains, they lose creativity
Then everywhere there is anarchy
So the true souls try for democracy
Then you will see the true beauty
The active souls make good society
Good society means, all are happy
So every time "Change is necessary"

Meaning:

Our soul has to be active. Our hidden strength has to come out and make the people aware. If the people are silent, there will be a huge loss to the society.

104. Our School (TMRS Jangaon-Boys-1)

The biodiversity is seen in our

school premises, it is the wonderful

place as you can see the dissimilar

animal species, the weather is cool

The birds' chirping, Peacocks' roaming, and frogs'

jumping, multi insects, diverse types of

plants and you come across poisonous snakes

What other than this makes a beautiful life?

My students discuss about a leopard

the villagers have seen there, they also

enjoy to look at a herd of deer and

a warren of rabbits' leap is like choreo

We are very fortunate to have such

gorgeous, stunning premises to encroach

Meaning:

The poem talks about our school, TMRS JANGAON BOYS-1. Our school is situated in the lap of nature. You can multi-species of animals of birds and animals. It is the best of biodiversity.

105. Roller Bird

Indian Roller Bird is Telangana state bird
To see it, people on Dusserah are gathered
They move to the places in the countryside
After seeing the bird, the people are satisfied
Seeing it is treated as a harbinger of good luck
It is a belief on this day Pandavas came back
For Dusserah, the Jambi tree became a landmark
The people pluck the leaves and speak and shriek
Even the enemies become friends on this day
They forget their enmity at the end of day
They go back to their house in the green way
At the dusk, their happiness is taken away

Meaning:

Indian Roller is the state's bird. People see it on Dussehra. They believe good things happen when they see it on the festival. It was said even pandavas saw it and won in the battle.

106. Agriculture is our culture

Agriculture is our culture
It is India's prime feature
Without it, there's no future
Agriculture is part of nature
India is a place of farmers
Farmers are the living gods
They yield food to populace
So all are living in happiness
Farming is the art of living
A farmer is spiritual being
Spirituality is a nice feeling
It never gets you boring

Meaning:

Agriculture is our culture and it is Indian quality. It is the way of living spiritual life. People without food can't live. So farmers are the living gods.

107. Fuedal system came to end

Fuedal system came to end
Plutocracy has established
No change in the livelihood
Age made the life wretched
Labourer became instrument
In politics, farmer was caught
Weaver failed in latest market
The artists live without paint
Now everyone needs guidance
to live the life without distress
The writers can give suggestions
Thus they can change the lives

Meaning:

In this competitive world, it is becoming very tough to lead life though all the evils have gone out like feudalism, plutocracy. Only writers can give good suggestions to live the life in the best way.

108. Dyspeptic Books

Dyspeptic books are worried
because they are only carried
but not properly used or read
In the racks, they are decorated
Carrying books without reading
is like a buried dead body's living
Wake up from the rustic thinking
and stop stereotype of working
Work hard, do something useful
Otherwise life is not meaningful
Never be remorseful, resentful
Be strong, life will be wonderful

Meaning:

Why to study books without digesting them. The people mostly decorate them by keeping in the racks. They are to read not to buried.

Epilogue

I feel very blessed to write Thrilling Telangana- Candid Culture and Customs. With utmost love and respect on my state, I completed this book. The grand history of Telangana made me to write this book. And the most important thing is its people and the greatness of them. The fighting spirit in non violent way brought the separate state. The same spirit of the government stood the small state in the top in all aspects in the short time. After the state is separated, its dialect, culture, cuisines and all other things are revived. I finally request the readers to know the culture and heritage of our state in my poems. The poems are composed in poetic style with proper rhyming and figurative language. I hope my hard work will be paid back in the form of recognition.

Konda Murali

Author and Poet

9441431090

mahabhi1310@gmail.com